Deepening Faith
To Know and Be Known

Participant's Guide

New Life Lutheran Church in Dripping Springs, TX (altar pictured) uses mustang grapes on the church land to make sacramental wine with labels often designed by the children. This welcome Table reminds us of the tables we gather at To Know and Be Known.

Mindy Roll

ISBN-13: 978-0692933084 (Texas-Louisiana Gulf Coast Synod, The)
ISBN-10: 0692933085

And let us consider how to provoke one another to love and good deeds,
not neglecting to meet together, as is the habit of some,
but encouraging one another,
and all the more as you see the day approaching.

Hebrews 10:24-25

ACKNOWLEDGMENTS

Many thanks to Janelle Rozek Hooper, Michael Rinehart,
and the Gulf Coast Synod staff for making this possible.

CONTENTS

WELCOME!

Greetings Deepening Faith Community Groups!

Welcome to *Deepening Faith: To Know and Be Known*. Deepening Faith is the Gulf Coast Synod's initiative to grow and deepen faith throughout our synod, in our churches, individuals, and neighborhoods. This initiative grew out of the refrain we began to hear among members and leaders: Help us to experience faith more fully and more deeply.

Over the next year, your small group will have the opportunity to get to know one another in a new way, explore faith together, and deepen your understanding of prayer, discipleship, and justice.

But to do this well, we must begin with our stories.

The first 8 weeks of our time together will be focused on deepening relationships within the group. Each member will have the opportunity to reflect on and share their story with one another. Sound intimidating? It is, but just a little bit – and we will help you learn how to do this.

Following the first eight weeks, groups will be able to decide their own direction, choosing units in: Spirituality & Prayer; Justice & Service; Scripture & Theology; Worship; and the Language of Faith. Our hope is that at the end of each unit, you will have come to a deeper and more robust understanding of faith and the ways that God is moving among you and your group.

As part of this curriculum, you will have the opportunity to take a Faith Assessment. It's not a test, we promise! Rather, it's a tool to help you understand where you are on your faith journey and where you would like to grow. You will be invited to re-take the assessment throughout your time in small groups, noticing how your faith has deepened while being part of this community.

We pray that this regular way of gathering is transformative for you and your group.

So welcome to the journey!

Mindy Roll

GROUP GUIDELINES
Together, we commit to the following:

Trust/Sharing. Members are encouraged to share on a deeper level than they might initially feel comfortable doing. This helps us to truly know and trust one another.

Vulnerability. For growth to happen in faith, each participant must choose to be a little vulnerable. Stretch yourself to share the harder things in your lives.

Strict Confidentiality. Anything shared in the group stays in the group unless a member has the express permission of the sharer to share outside of the group.

Introverts & Extroverts. This group is likely composed of some who are introverts (listen more than speak) and extroverts (speak more than listen). A good balance of voices includes introverts pushing themselves to process aloud, and extroverts challenging themselves to listen more than speak.

Group Conversation. Pay attention to your own contribution in group conversation. Are you speaking more or less than others? A good rule of thumb is to allow each person to speak once or twice, but then to hold off until all members have shared.

Listening to Stories. As we listen to one another's stories, we may be tempted to jump in with advice or similar stories, which we may do in normal conversation. Please hold off on immediately responding to one another, using the group format of Thanks/Because as a means of response.

"Faith-Ing" Other's Stories. Sometimes well-intentioned people want to "faith" other's stories, that is help them interpret them through Scripture which can be received as corrective or even dismissive.

Commitment. Small Groups require a fairly high level of commitment. Certainly things come up which are unavoidable and require missing a night. As possible, however, please plan on missing no more than 1-2 nights each session. If this guideline feels too difficult, it might not be the right time to join a small group.

Resources. It's possible you may come across things that need additional processing. Know that your pastor is available and can also refer you to others who can process with you on a deeper level (for example, a licensed therapist or a spiritual director).

1 THE INITIAL GATHERING

Welcome to Session 1! At tonight's gathering, you will begin to get to know your fellow small group participants. You will spend some time discussing your group's covenant, as well as identifying a prayer practice for your group to commit to together for the next eight weeks. You will watch a video of Bishop Mike introducing you to this journey and sharing his own story. You will also set your group's schedule and learn about the Faith Assessment.

For the next three weeks, we will focus on learning how to hear others' stories, as well as learning how to tell your own. To learn how to tell your own, you will have homework each week, which can be written or talked about (or both). When it comes time to tell *your* story to the group – in a short 15 minutes – you'll have created an outline through your homework.

Homework

This week's homework will focus on your earliest years, recalling three memories that have had a significant impact on who you have become.

Begin by reading Psalm 139:1-18, reflecting on what it means that God has known you from the very beginning of your life, even before you were known to yourself or your family.

Then spend some time reflecting, and then writing about these three questions. Consider talking with family about these topics.

1. For the first question, think about the life that you were born into. Were you the oldest, the youngest, or somewhere in the middle? Were you a surprise or were you long-awaited? Did you grow up in your birth family, extended family, or adopted family? Did your family struggle financially, or was your family comfortable? What was happening in the world when you were born? What were the patterns that lived in your family – alcoholism, abuse, physical or mental illness, poverty, loved ones returning from war? Perhaps there were more positive practices as well - eating meals together, weekly church, visiting grandparents? For the first question, paint a picture of the home you were born into.

2. For the second question, write about a defining moment in your childhood. Perhaps there was an early loss in your family or perhaps there was an occasion that brought great joy. What stands out as you think about school, friendships, family, your home, and how you learned to see the world at a young age?

3. For the third question, write about a "becoming" moment, where you realized something significant about who you were. Perhaps you felt a "call" to a certain person, work, or role; perhaps becoming married/partnered or a parent changed significant things about you; perhaps you realized something significant about who God created you to be. What happened in your young adult years to help you become who you are now?

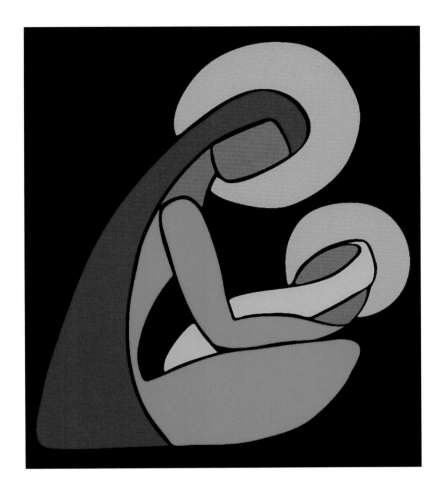

2 INTRODUCING STORIES

Welcome to Session 2! At tonight's gathering, we will hear your pastor's faith story and spend some time in conversation about what resonated with your own story.

Following the evening, reflect on this question: What did you notice about how your pastor's story was shared?

Homework

This week's homework will focus on the high points in your story, the moments or periods where you felt most alive, connected, and proud.

Begin by reading Luke 1:39-55, reflecting on Mary's story, including the great joy she felt at the pronouncement that she would be the mother of Jesus. What has great joy looked like in your life?

Then spend some time writing or talking about these questions:

1. For the first question, call to mind a period in your life where you met someone who would change the course of who you were becoming. This might be a teacher, mentor, romantic partner, "soul friend," or anyone else who has had a significant impact on you. Write about that period in your life and how they influenced you. How are you different because of them?

2. For the second question, call to mind a period in your life where you felt "your cup runneth over." Perhaps you did not recognize it at the time (and perhaps nostalgia is making it more perfect than it actually was), but in retrospect, you see it as a period of much joy and gladness. What made this so?

3. For the third question, call to mind a period in your life where you felt like your contribution mattered greatly. Perhaps you were studying or doing work that you loved, or were involved in significant justice or service work, or you were caring for others. Why was this an important period for you? What did it tell you about who you are?

3 GROUP LEADERS' STORIES

Welcome to Session 3! At tonight's gathering, we will hear your small group leaders' stories.
This week we shift to listening to stories in person, and your small group leaders will be the first to share. As you listen tonight, remember the ground rules that small groups have been asked to follow: Hold confidentiality, don't rush to respond, and be a little vulnerable.

A note on listening. Perhaps a friend in your life has given you a hard time about not listening closely. Perhaps you *were* actually listening, but your friend could not tell that based on your body language. So here's a few tips: Hold eye contact. If your mind starts to wander, take notes. Lean forward. Uncross your arms. Turn off your phone. This shows the group that we are serious about hearing one another's stories well.

Recognize that sharing makes us vulnerable and that someone is feeling vulnerable right now. If the sharer gets teary or emotional, don't rush to "make it less awkward" or fill the silence, but give them space to continue. A pat on the back or a hand squeeze goes a long way, if the sharer welcomes that.

After each sharer, you will have some time to reflect and fill in the Thanks/Because sentence that you will speak back to one another. An example of a Thanks/Because Response might be: *Thank you for sharing about the impact that your father had on you because it helped me realize that I'm not the only one who struggles with my dad.* Or *Thank you for sharing about the time you walked away from the church; I never knew that part of your story, and I can now see why it's important.*

Small Group Leader #1:

What struck you about this story?

Thank you for sharing/because....

Small Group Leader #2:

What struck you about this story?

Thank you for sharing/because....

Homework

This week's homework will focus on the low points in your story, or the moments or periods you felt the most disconnected, down, confused, or lost.

Begin by reading Psalm 42, reflecting on times when your soul has felt "cast down" or when tears have "been your food day and night."

Then spend some time reflecting and writing about these questions:

1. For the first question, call to mind the hardest period of grief in your life. Perhaps you lost a parent, grandparent, spouse/partner, sibling, or child. Perhaps it was the loss of a relationship, job, or home. Perhaps it was the loss of your idealism or naïveté. Who/what did you lose and what was this period like for you?

2. For the second question, call to mind a time when you forgot who you were. Perhaps you were involved in a job or relationship that caused you to act unlike yourself. Perhaps a change of roles in your life proved difficult to come to terms with. Perhaps the change was a good, but painful one. How did you come back to yourself?

3. For the third question, call to mind the hardest transition in your life. Perhaps you are still in it now and that has helped shaped your desire to be in a small group. Perhaps the transition was a necessary one, but one that has been harder than you anticipated. What happened during this transition and how are you different because of it?

4 PARTICIPANTS' STORIES ONE

Welcome to Sessions 4-7!

Beginning in week 4, we get to hear one another's stories. For the next four weeks, our small group will follow the same format. Each week three people will share their story

The week before you share your story, you will be invited to do the following exercise to prepare. (Note: If you are sharing during week four [good for you!], you'll need to do week's four homework and the exercise below during week 3.)

Homework the week before you share your story:

Review your first four weeks of writing about your story (this will include this week's homework). When it comes time to share your story, you will have 15 minutes (which will fly by) to share the significant things about your life. You do not need to share all 12 things that you wrote down (you'd have to be a speed talker to share all that in 15 minutes!). Instead, you might think about your story like this:

The world & family you were born into (3 minutes)
A formative event from your childhood/adolescence (3 minutes)
A significant high in your life (3 minutes)
A significant low in your life (3 minutes)
How faith has been part of or not part of your life (3 minutes)

The key: Be honest and be real. The groups wants to know *you*, not just the you you present to the world. Be a little vulnerable in sharing your story. It's okay if you get teary or emotional. That's vulnerability!

Practice your talk a few times for the sake of time, but recognize that the pieces you share may change in the moment as the Holy Spirit guides you. Your group leader will give you a 5-minute warning, then a 2-minute warning, which should help you keep your story within 15 minutes.

Thank you for sharing your story. Know that there are a whole network of folks who are praying for you tonight!

Also starting this week, your homework will involve two things. The first is beginning the Faith Assessment, which is at the end of your booklet. This will need to be completed before Session 8.

The second piece of homework will involve writing affirmations for your fellow group members. During Session 8, you will have the opportunity to write a message of support, affirmation, and discernment to each member. It will be helpful to have thought about or written out what you want to write prior to Session 8.

A good affirmation sees beneath the surface. What do you notice - really notice - about this person, their gifts, their faith, and their way of being in the world?

A thoughtful affirmation may look like this: *You see the world with so much depth. I appreciate your kindness, warmth, and compassion for others. I also appreciate how gentle you are with your children, and the patience you show toward others. I really value your presence in this group.*

Homework for next week: Telling Your Story: Faith & Meaning

This week's homework will be centered on recognizing God's presence, faith, and meaning in your story. This is the part of understanding our stories that some Christians find the most difficult. When asked to share their faith story, they might talk about church membership or the committees that they have been part of, struggling to articulate the ways that God is and has moved in their lives. Tonight's exercise asks you to be intentional in your reflection, looking at your story through a new lens.

Begin by reading Luke 24:13-27, reflecting on how Jesus helped the two disciples interpret what they had seen and experienced.

Then read back over the nine experiences you have written about over the last four weeks: three from your formative years; three highs; and three lows. Perhaps the movement of God in those stories stands out to you right away; perhaps not.

For tonight's assignment, pick three of the instances that you wrote about. As you bring to mind each story, ask yourself the following questions:

1. Christians often mistakenly await a lightning bolt or a sign from above to tell us that God is present. A deepening faith, however, reminds us that God often comes in more subtle ways: through a friend or loved one; through a feeling of peace; through the church community; through the sacraments. As you look back over your three stories, how might you see that God was actually present in subtle ways?

2. Our faith reminds us that we do not believe that God makes bad things happen to test our faith or make us stronger or punish us. We do believe, however, that God can bring meaning and hope to even the darkest situations of our lives. As you look back over a darker period in your life, what meaning or hope has emerged that you did not see initially?

3. Our faith reminds us that all good things come from God. As you look back over your life, what has been an unexpected "good thing" that has emerged when you did not expect it? How did this help you to know God?

Session 4 Stories:

What struck you about the stories shared tonight?

Thank you for sharing /because….

Thank you for sharing/because…

Homework:

Affirmation for:

Affirmation for:

Affirmation for:

5 PARTICIPANTS' STORIES TWO

Welcome to session 5!

This week, as last week, we will be listening as participants share their stories. If you are sharing your story next week, be sure to complete **Homework the week before you share your story** (page 24) the week before you share your story.

What struck you about the stories shared tonight?

Thank you for sharing /because....

Thank you for sharing/because...

Homework:

Affirmation for:

Affirmation for:

Affirmation for:

6 PARTICIPANTS' STORIES THREE

Welcome to session 6!

This week, as last week, we will be listening as participants share their stories. If you are sharing your story next week, be sure to complete **Homework the week before you share your story** (page 24) the week before you share your story.

What struck you about the stories shared tonight?

Thank you for sharing /because....

Thank you for sharing/because...

Homework:

Affirmation for:

Affirmation for:

Affirmation for:

7 PARTICIPANTS' STORIES FOUR

Welcome to session 7!

This week, as last week, we will be listening as participants share their stories. If you are sharing your story next week, be sure to complete **Homework the week before you share your story** (page 24) the week before you share your story.

What struck you about the stories shared tonight?

Thank you for sharing /because….

Thank you for sharing/because…

Homework:

Affirmation for:

Affirmation for:

Affirmation for:

8 CELEBRATING STORIES

Welcome to Session 8!

Tonight is our final week together in the story-telling portion of Deepening Faith. We will spend part of our time writing affirmations and part of our time in conversation around the Faith Assessment. Before we get to the Faith Assessment, though, reflect on where you've been together as a group. How does tonight's dinner conversation feel different than week one's?

Following tonight, your group may take a break before either going on retreat together or beginning the next curriculum. Consider how you might stay in touch as a group, supporting and encouraging one another, praying for each other, and being a source of love in each other's lives.

Tonight, based on the conversation around the Faith Assessment, your group may choose your next direction. Some options include:

- Spirituality & Prayer

- Justice & Service

- Scripture & Theology

- Worship

- Language of Faith

Thank you for taking this initial journey into deeper faith. We hope that it has deepened your understanding of God's presence in your life, both in your story and through the members of your small group.

AFFIRMATIONS PAGE

Write your name here_____ **and pass this page around!**

FAITH ASSESSMENT

Faith

Pick which description(s) most closely match how you would describe FAITH

1. My faith is simple, trusting, and black-and-white. There is a right or wrong answer for most questions. My faith is unbothered by larger questions about the world.
2. My faith has a lot of questions (for example, how do we reconcile science and faith? How do we understand scripture around sexuality? How do we believe in miracles when experience tells us otherwise?).
3. My faith used to have a lot of questions, but when I saw that the church/my community wasn't interested in them, I began to step away. So I am sort of involved, but I am not sure that I buy all the "church stuff."
4. My faith is more nuanced than it used to be and often operates in shades of gray. There is rarely a right or wrong answer, but often a faithful approach.
5. I am satisfied with where I am in my faith journey.
6. I would like to grow in my faith journey.
7. I am not sure about all this faith talk. I thought faith was something you either had or did not have.

In your own words, describe your faith:

In your own words, describe the faith you hope to grow into:

Prayer & Spirituality

Pick which description(s) most closely match how you would describe prayer:
1. Prayer is a process of telling God what you need. Regular prayer might include confession, thanksgiving, and supplication (asking God for what you need).
2. Prayer is a process of learning to listen for God. Regular prayer might include silence, meditation, walking, or writing.
3. Prayer is a rhythm of thanking God throughout the day. Regular prayer might include morning prayer, mealtime prayers, and bedtime prayers.
4. Prayer is a recognition of the way God comes to you most profoundly. Regular prayer might include deep conversation with a friend, time with loved ones, or being in a space that brings you joy.
5. Prayer is a discipline. You must develop it.
6. Prayer is a gift. You must receive it.
7. I have no idea. Prayer is a mystery to me, one I don't understand well.

In your own words, describe your understanding of prayer, including how you currently pray (if you do - it's ok if you don't):

In your own words, describe the prayer you hope to grow into, including prayer in your home:

Justice & Service

"Justice" is a concept that shows up in both society and scripture often. Take a stab at defining justice:

Christians believe that service to our neighbor is an important part of discipleship. Think back over the last year. List the service work you have been engaged in. Then reflect: is this more or less than you thought you had been engaged in? What is a rhythm of service that you would like for yourself (and/or your family)?

On a scale of 1-10, how confident do you feel articulating a faith-filled approach to each of the following:
1. Immigration   _____
2. Racism   _____
3. Hunger & Poverty   _____
4. Sexuality   _____
5. The Environment   _____
6. Gender   _____
7. Disability   _____

Which of those do you find hardest to understand from a faith perspective?

Scripture and Theology

Mark True/False/Meh for the following:

1. When Scripture is read on Sunday mornings in church, I sit up and take good notes. This is good stuff!
2. When Scripture is read on Sunday mornings in church, I sorta pay attention and sorta make my grocery list. Why on earth are we reading from Obadi-who?
3. I read and study the Bible regularly in my home. This is good stuff!
4. Our family Bible is an excellent paperweight. I think. Actually, I'm not sure where it is.
5. Reading the Bible is challenging because I am not sure how to do it. Where do I even start? How do I interpret it? What does it mean in today's context? Without knowing that sort of stuff, I'm not even sure how to begin.
6. Being in Bible Study has changed my life.
7. If a non-Christian asked me to talk about the Bible, I could confidently walk them through our basic approach to Scripture, our understanding of broad themes, what we mean by Law & Gospel, the concept of scripture interpreting scripture, and what we mean by a text pointing to Christ.
8. I would like to know how to study and be engaged with Scripture.

In your own words, how do you feel about the Bible?

Worship

I attend worship on Sundays because (be honest):

The most meaningful part of Sunday worship is (be honest):

When I leave worship, I feel (be honest):

Lutheran Christians believe that worship is the movement of God coming to meet us through: the gathered community, the sacraments, the scripture and proclamation (sermon), the songs and music -- and then sending us into the world. Does this match your Sunday experience? How or how not?

Language of Faith

Most Christians would agree that the following statements are not true and inconsistent with our faith. How would you, using the language of your own faith, respond to the following assertions:

Christians from other traditions are going to hell!

You must personally accept Jesus Christ into your heart to be saved.

Only men should speak in church.

Racism has nothing to do with faith and the church.

SCHEDULE AND LOCATION

Session 1   Date and time:

Host: Address & Phone:

Session 2   Date and time:

Host: Address & Phone:

Session 3   Date and time:

Host: Address & Phone:

Session 4   Date and time:

Host: Address & Phone:

Session 5   Date and time:

Host: Address & Phone:

Session 6   Date and time:

Host: Address & Phone:

Session 7   Date and time:

Host: Address & Phone:

Session 8   Date and time:

Host: Address & Phone:

ABOUT THE AUTHOR

Mindy Roll is the Pastor at Treehouse, the Lutheran (ELCA) Campus Ministry at Texas A&M and Blinn College, where she has served since 2010. Mindy is a graduate of Texas A&M, Yale Divinity School, the Lutheran Theological Seminary at Gettysburg, and is currently enrolled at Brite Divinity School. When not pondering the world with college students, Mindy and her husband Tom are sprinting after their two small children, Andrew and Linden.